A collaborative
Poetry Writing Project

This book is dedicated to my Mum "Gwen'ma", who helps me with all my ventures and who is my first and favourite teacher.

Written & Illustrated by
19 Amazing Young Poets

# WHY THE PROJECT?

I loved writing as a child and have encouraged the same in my children. I have four little creative people of my own who I home educate and we share our home educating journey and resources through our website KyndaKids.com. I love the fact that I'm able to give my children a platform like this to create and write poetry and to share this opportunity with others.

When Covid-19 caused a world-wide lockdown, Forester Financials offered funding to its members to enable us to make a meaningful impact in our communities while social distancing. From a writer's perspective, what could be more meaningful than to get 19 young 'poets' to write an inspirational book of poetry?

So I created "Poems KNOW", a collaborative poetry writing project that brings together young, up-and-coming poets.

I hope to run more writing projects through Kynda Kids in the future and create more poets and story writers in the process.

Kylie Thompson
Mother of Kynda Kids

# WHAT IS A POEM?

Poetry is a collection of words
put together to be read or heard
They convey emotion, ideas and such
creative and detailed no words are too much.

So many styles and ways to be written,
poetry is one of the first things we're given
Through song and through rhyme,
be it nursery or pop.
Our learning of words
Will never stop.

Funny or not, short or long,
no poem you write can ever be wrong.
Your words, your feelings
and all of your meanings
are yours to be shared,
so don't be scared.

Serious or sad,
descriptive, but never bad,
poems are the best way
to express what you want to say.

Poems can, but don't have to rhyme;
some have a rhythm, that you sing in time.
They can help you to see
with creative imagery.
With 19 poets to introduce you to
Please enjoy this book I created for you!

By Kylie (35)

# Corona Virus

**C**orona virus taking over the planet

**O**pportunity to stay at home and spend time with family

**R**ainbows and clapping for the NHS

**O**h no there are no toilet rolls!

**N**o schools or clubs

**A** new way of life

**V**irus spreading fast

**I** wish I could hug my friends and family

**R**emember the two meter rule!

**U**sing computer to stay connected

**S**aving the planet.

By Hannah (8)

# My cat Monty

I got a cat in lockdown
His name is Monty and he
likes to roll in the sun
He snores like my dad
and annoys my mum
Sometimes he falls off
the sofa and I laugh
But I want to give him a
warm and lovely bath

I was very bored in
lockdown but
The cat snuggles up to me
And makes me crazily happy

Purrrrrr
Meow meoooooooow....

By Lucas (11)

## Be Happy

This virus is letting some people down,
I should be unhappy and wearing a frown
But I am happy on lockdown.
I am missing my friends
And they're missing me too
But we can still FaceTime like we always do.
There is skipping and running and my bicycle too,
Reading and writing and homework to do.
Don't be sad, try and be happy on lockdown too.

By Ava (8)

# Quarantine surprise

There once was a virus called COVID nineteen
So everyone in the world had to be in quarantine
It was hard to get things done
And nothing was fun
It changed everyone to a boring routine

# Boring!

Quarantine was boring, most of the time, I was snoring, now playing lego is boring, I don't like snoring, everything is boring,
I want to be out walking.

By Kyle (7)

# Joem

After quarantine we'll be happy
Because we make ginger snacks
So everyone will be clappy
And change all of the facts
By giving the world party packs

By Jordan (5)

# Coronavirus, the annoying bug.

Hey bug, you spoil everybody's fun,
I wish I could throw you to the sun!
Tie you up, so you can't escape,
then throw you into space.
I wish I can do that, but you are invisible,
That's why you are unstoppable.
So I just wanted to go to pets at home,
I didn't want to think about you anymore.
There I was very lucky,
As I got a hamster called Carlie.

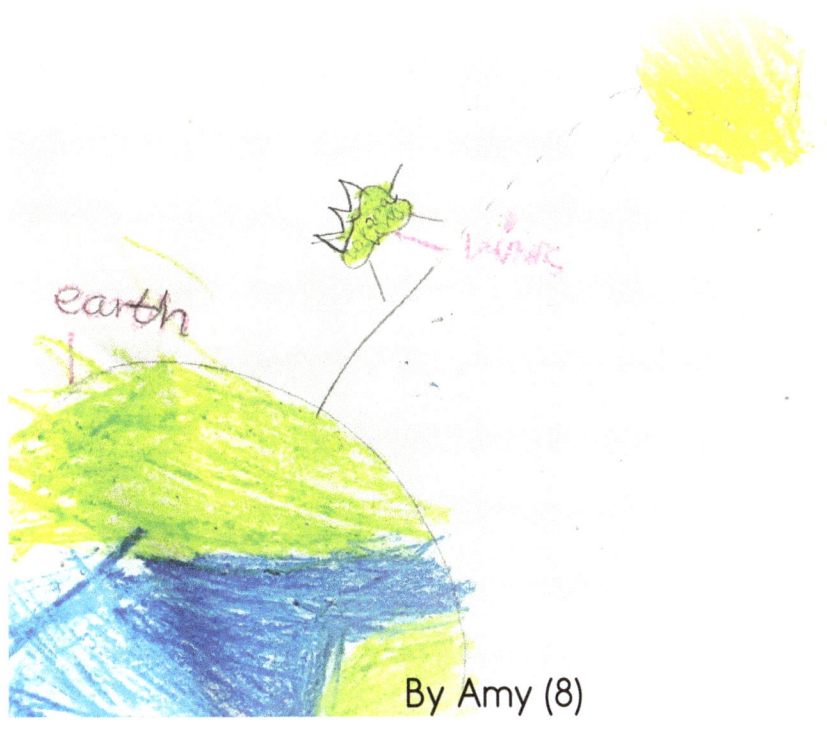

By Amy (8)

# Coronavirus

Coronavirus you are everywhere,
Under the table and under the chair.
On a person on a bat,
on a really stinky hat,

You are in a house,
You are on a door,
And you are on the number four.

You shut down schools,
You shut down shops,
Especially sweet shops with lollypops.

Lots of places where people gather,
Look really dull
and more boring than climbing a never-ending ladder.

So Coronavirus,
Wherever you may be,
everyone hates you,
even a dirty flea!

By Ryan (10)

# Joshua's Poem

I don't like Coronavirus
It's so boring,
There is nothing to do.
Quarantine is the worst
We can't go outside,
Can't go to the playground.
It's boring at home
I need something to do
I want to go to somebody's house.

When Corona started I stopped going to school
I miss my friends but we still talk online.
Everything has changed
People queue to go to the shops
Playgrounds are closed
You're only allowed to go outside when you need to go to the shop or park and exercise
During this time I kept busy and had fun going to the park and having picnics and playing football
I hope everyone stayed safe and everything is normal again soon.

By Joshua (9)

# Spreading Corona
## - A Haiku Poem

In China people
Started to worry about
Coronavirus

It began to spread
England, Italy, US
No country was spared

Then what happened is
People were locked down worldwide
It was terrible.

By Lucy (7)

# Life Inside

Since Corona started things have only gotten worse

But does that mean it's that much of a bubble burst?

Think of it in a good way you're stuck at home hidden away from a cruel bad world with your family so why must we frown when you look through the window and into the clouds
You see people wearing masks - you have even stronger fabric: You're protected by a house!

Think of this as a blessing think of the things you might find out you might be a good cook

Maybe sing and shout all the things you might find out

So please don't take your life inside as a punishment it is a blessing!

By Shalomie (9)

# My Side of Covid

Covid 19 is really killing me

I really really want to be free

Why can't I just go run around

Nowadays its so boring in town

It does stop me from swimming in pools diving away like nothing before

All the masks and medicines people take

It all gives me a huge headache

Thank you for listening to my side of the story,

because at the end of the day there is always glory.

By Shakari (7)

# Noah's Poem

I've lived through a pandemic,
but I did not panic
I wash my hands more
but it's kind of a bore
I'm really quite happy,
sometimes a bit flappy
I have to stay 2 metres away,
I wish it would delay
Can't wait to see my friends,
whenever this ends
I'm bored of Corona,
I wish it was over!

By Noah (6)

# Corona virus

**C**hina is where it all began

**O**rdering online, the only way to shop

**R**eady, the opposite of what England was

**O**ld folk at risk and to care homes it spread

**N**o school to teach

**A**irlines grounded, nowhere to fly

**V**accine the only thing they wish

**I**solating, no joy for those living alone

**R**uthless this coronavirus is

**U**seless we are, all stuck at home

**S**ymptoms not always noticeable, when will it end?

best friends: rabies, sars, ebola, black death, bumn colds, flu.

←2m→

hobbies: killing, mak ing people ill, banning travel
best hobby: doing lockdowns.

By Katie (8)

# Alana's Poem

Daffodils are small
Daffodils are bright
Daffodils are even in the moonlight

Try and find them in spring
I'm sure you can
because they're beautiful just like a lamb

This Spring was different
Lockdown made it quieter
But daffodils grew stronger, and prettier and brighter

Daffodils grow from a seed
To a tall lovely flower
They love to be close to each other
Daffodils smell sweet like vanilla

Daffodils have long green stems
And a lovely centre called a cup,
The daffodils rise up like the sun
Like we will rise up when the lockdown is done

By Alana (8)

# This Beastly Lockdown

The Spanish Flu was quite a disaster,
Thank goodness it went and wasn't a laster,
The Ebola disease was pretty bad too,
Closely following a SARS-induced flu.

But no recent disease was quite so widespread,
(And half a million people are dead),
For the people living through Covid-19,
Their Christmas list has one word – vaccine.

Earth was hit by a thing called a lockdown,
The planet's economy has gone into breakdown,
But though some on earth have had it quite bad,
Us little children are stuck home and sad.

Isolated each day with nothing to do,
Without all our friends because of this flu,
Then, in March, at the government's insistence,
We couldn't even see our own grandparents!

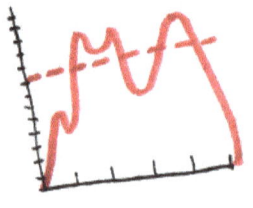

We did all our school work at home every day,
And my friends couldn't come for my birthday!
It was like this for months, this staying inside,
Two meters apart was the rule to abide.

I couldn't go to dancing, I couldn't do gym,
I couldn't go swimming, I had to stay in!
Holidays, funfairs were also a no-no,
Playgrounds and soft plays, more places I can't go.

But there was one thing I really missed most,
Not seeing my friends, not getting close,
The playdates and such I couldn't attend,
This beastly lockdown, oh why won't it end!

By Sophie (11)

# My Big Sister

I'm really happy

That in lock down

I get to spend more time

With my big sis Tay

We never get to play

But it's good the time I have

Because it may never happen again

My big sister is a teenager

A very moody one indeed

Now this is the end of the poem

You'll see the next one soon

So talk to you under the moon

By Tiahni "SweetTee" (11)

# Josiah's Poem

One time, on an ordinary day I woke up,

looked at the news and everything's corrupt.

Shelves were empty, can't go to school.

Beaches full, sadly things were not cool.

People wearing masks, having to stand 2 meters away.

Now I cant go to an area to play.

Boris got trapped in mayhem, like people saying "hey!?!"

People saying "who!?!" People saying "man this is worse than the flu".

NHS work away. The rainbow, a sign that they save the day.

I can't wait to see my friends, when this virus finally comes to an end.

By Josiah (8)

# The Scoot Olympics

Today is the Scoot Olympics
where everyone scoots

The person who wins it, gets a lot of loot

All wheels accepted, wheels big and small

Not as big as a car but maybe something tall

But there's a little girl who's
scooted with all her might

And there inside herself she found a little light

So she scooted and scooted
and went on to win the race

Then her sister appeared and said "you should
have seen your face"

That's why I try and try and try with all my might

And every time I doubt myself
I see that little light.

By Aimee (9)

# Taylah's Poem

Living in lockdown
is hard for some
who try to recover
but the damage is done.

Many live through it
but others don't,
some will be ready
but others won't.

We should help each other,
whatever it takes.
Be on the right side
of the history being made.

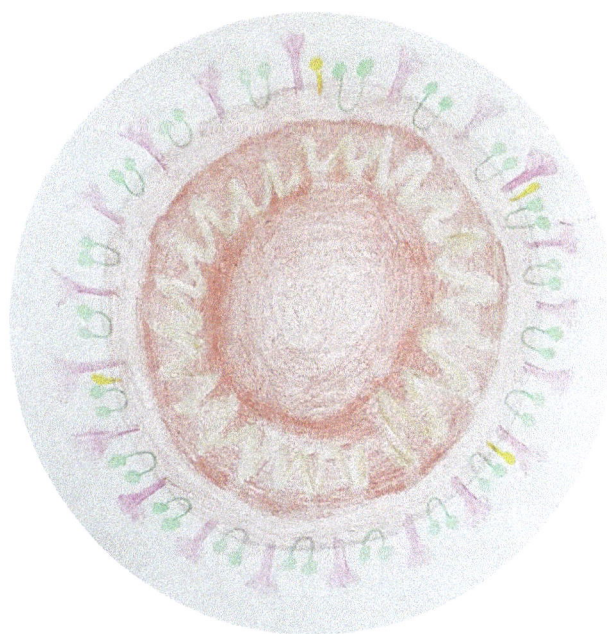

By Taylah (13)

# Types of Poems

## Rhymed

Most people expect poetry to rhyme. Typically, rhymed poetry is quatrain. Rhyming couplets are formal verses that take on a rhyming scheme.

Popular rhyme schemes are AABB CCDD (rhyming the first and second line and then the third and fourth) or ABAB CDCD (rhyming the first and third and the second and fourth line). The rhymed poem does not have to stick to one rhyming format.

## Free Verse

A poem that does not take on the traditional poem structure. There's no pattern, consistent rhyme or musical form and usually reads as an improvised speech. It would normally be recited in the way that we would naturally speak.

## LIMERICK

Funny and sometimes even rude poems with an AABBA rhyming scheme. The BB lines are shorter than the others and limericks usually have a familiar musical rhythm.

## ACROSTIC

A poem that uses the first letter of every line to spell out a word relating to the topic.

## CINQUAIN

A Poem with five lines and no rhyme scheme.

## HAIKU

A haiku is a Japanese style poem, using three-line stanza. The first line has five syllables, the second line has seven syllables, and the third line again has five syllables.

## HUMOROUS

A poem that is funny or silly. It can rhyme and is fun to read.

## CONCRETE
A poem that takes the shape of an image of the poems theme.

## BIO
A poem that describes a person, famous or made up.

## BALLAD
A poem that tells a serious story and usually rhymes.

# GLOSSARY

**ALLITERATION** using words that have the same starting sound.

**CINQUAIN** a five-line stanza.

**COUPLET** A two-line stanza.

**METER** the pattern of stressed syllables (long-sounding) and unstressed syllables (short-sounding) in poetry.

**MONOSTICH** A poem or stanza with just one line.

**ONOMATOPOEIA** is the use of a word or words that sound like what they are meant to represent. I.e. Buzz, hiss.

**QUATRAIN** a four-line stanza.

**RHYME SCHEME** the pattern of rhyme that comes at the end of each line or verse. E.g. cat and hat or giggle and riddle.

**RHYTHM** Rhythm is the beat or movement of a line. This includes the rise and fall of an unstressed syllable followed by a stressed syllable.

**SESTET** a six-line stanza.

**SIMILES** is a form of figure of speech that uses the word like or as to compare two things that are similar.

**SONNET** A sonnet is a poem containing fourteen lines that rhyme.

**STANZA** A set amount of lines in poetry grouped together by their length, meter or rhyme scheme.

**SYLLABLE** the single, unbroken sound of a spoken or written word.

**TERCET** a three-line stanza.

# ABOUT THE POETS

I don't have one favourite thing to do but I do like reading stories that have happy endings and playing board games with our family. What makes me happy? Winning! I love reading about different characters and their exciting adventures.

Aimee Dunbar | Age 10 | pg. 22

Alana is 6 years old and loves animals. Her favourite thing to do is horse-riding. The things that make her most happy are playing with her cousins, and eating ice-cream!! She enjoys reading because non-fiction is interesting and she learns lots of facts. She enjoys fiction books because they are fun and enjoyable.

Alana Forde | Age 6 | pg. 17

Amy loves singing, making up musical stories, and playing with her friends. (she is missing her friends so much). She is very happy when she performs to her family at home. Amy likes reading fiction stories and stories about animals. She always wanted a pet and finally, she got her first-ever pet, a Hamster, called Charlie.

Amy Ilmane | Age 8 | pg. 9

Ava loves to ride her bike and learnt to ride a two wheeler very quickly. Food makes her happy and she loves to eat pizza. Ava finds reading books exciting and is currently reading, 'My Little Pony! Equestria Girls - Through the Mirror.

Ava Joseph-Burne | Age 7 | pg. 6

My favourite thing to do is to see my friends and play with animals. Doing crafty things, singing and music makes me feel happy. I enjoy reading books and listening to audio books as they take you on a magical journey.

Hannah Jenkings | Age 8 | pg. 4

My favourite thing to do is bake cakes and eat them! I'm happy when I get to play with my family, but mostly make cakes and save some for tomorrow. I like books because they're sometimes short and they have pictures.

Jordan Thompson | Age 5 | pg. 8

I enjoy playing Lego and building new sets which I usually get for Xmas and my birthday. Going out for food and seeing family, especially my little cousins makes me happy. I enjoy fantasy books and discovering the story the more you read.

Joshua Lyseight-Brown | Age 9 | pg. 11

My favourite thing to do is play with Lego. Reading books about animals makes me happy. I enjoy learning new things about animals when I read books.

Josiah Hall | Age 8 | pg. 21

Katie loves baking and her favourite animal is a snow leopard. In her free time she likes taking part in drama classes.

Katie Agmen-Smith | Age 9 | pg. 16

My favourite thing to do right now is to talk to people with video call, before quarantine it was playing Lego. In quarantine seeing people makes me happy but it used to be ice-cream and sour apples. I enjoy that books are very inspirational.

Kyle Thompson | Age 7 | pg. 7

Favourite thing to do: Be with my cat. What makes you happy: Being with my cat. What do you enjoy about books: using my imagination

Lucas Drury | Age 11 | pg. 5

Lucy loves ballet and playing with her puppy. She also likes playing the piano.

Lucy Agmen-Smith | Age 7 | pg. 12

My favourite thing is doing activities with mummy and playing! Being cuddled with mummy makes me happy and I like cuddling on the couch watching movies. Books can take you on wild adventures, and they tell good stories!

Noah Ogunleye | Age 6 | pg. 15

Ryan likes reading comic books, and making them. When he shows his finished movie or book to his family he is so happy. His love for books is not just reading them, but analysing them as well, for their value. He is helping a friend to list books on Abebooks site, and Ryan is so happy when he comes across a rare book during his research after he described and listed the book.

Ryan Ilmane | Age 10 | pg. 10

I like to exercise and I like to try different foods now. What makes me happy is when I'm calm and I SEE happiness. And last, I love books because most of them have a lovely ending like they live happily ever after or they get married.

Shakari Palmer | Age 7 | pg. 14

My favourite thing to do is cook. I like it when it's quiet and peaceful. I like the moral behind stories.

Shalomie Palmer | Age 9 | pg. 13

Sophie is a keen ballerina and hopes to be a full-time author in the future. She has already written her first novel and spends much of her free time reading.

Sophie Agmen-Smith | Age 11 | pg. 18

Taylah is a top-set student who loves school and lasagne. She hopes to be an actress when she grows up but wants to study law in university just in case. This would be the start of the path to her back-up plan of being a judge. Besides being intelligent and ambitious, Taylah helps to look after her three siblings and is also a form ambassador in her Student Union.

Taylah Sonia Anita Esson-Munroe | Age 13 | pg. 23

My favourite thing to do is chilling. My Mommy makes me happy and I enjoy books because they're funny.

Tiahni "SweetTee" Maria Esson-Munroe | Age 11 | pg. 20

www.ingramcontent.com/pod-product-compliance
Lightning Source LLC
Chambersburg PA
CBHW042000080526
44588CB00021B/2818